Life Skills Every 9 Year Old Should Know

Unlock Your Secret Superpowers and Succeed in All Areas of Life

Hayden Fox

4

Claim your free gifts!

(My way of saying thank you for your support)

Simply visit **haydenfoxmedia.com** to receive the following:

- 10 Powerful Dinner Conversations To Create Amazing Kids

- 10 Magical Affirmations To Help Kids Become Unstoppable in Life

(you can also scan this QR code)

This book belongs to

_____

Table of Contents

Introduction

Hey, kids! Do you sometimes wish that you could act more grown-up? Do you feel excited to learn how to do new things and stretch your growing independence? Many kids your age are excited to leave behind their childhood years and enter the tween and teen stages of life. Before you reach that point, there are some important life skills you need to know that will help you.

Perhaps you've already read *Life Skills for 8 Year Olds*; if so, that's great! You already know exactly what to expect in this book and how we'll approach brand-new life skills that will help you to keep growing and learn about being a good grown-up.

If you're new to the series, then welcome! This book is here to teach you twelve skills that will help you this year and for the rest of your life. There's a lot for you to learn, even though you're already nine years old, and that's a good thing! Having a lot to learn means you have a lot of room to grow, and growth is something that never stops. Even grown-ups continue to grow, learn, and get better at the things they practice.

As you read this book, you'll be introduced to lots of new skills. Some you might already be familiar with, and that's great! Hopefully, you'll still find some new information that will help you learn more. Other skills might be brand new to you and take some time to really learn and get used to.

The most important thing to remember as you read this book is that there's no reason to quit if things get tough. Sometimes, things are hard to learn and do; sometimes, you might feel defeated or angry about them. It's okay! The first skill we're going to look at is how to develop what I like to call a champion mindset. It's the mindset that will help you see that you can do anything you put your mind to, even if you fail at first.

Growing up can be hard. There's so much that you've already learned, and it can be hard to think about how much there is to learn out there. Just remember, there's always more you can learn. You can continue to develop your skills, and there's more that you can do to become a better person. As long as you keep working on these things and don't give up, you're doing great!

Whenever you feel stuck, or if something you find in this book is hard to think about or hard to understand, don't forget that the grown-ups in your life are there to help you. Before we begin diving into all the new skills for you to learn, I want you to stop for a minute and think of at least five grown-ups that you can talk to if you need help. They can be parents, aunts, uncles, grandparents, neighbors, teachers, or any other grown-ups you regularly see that you and your parents know and trust. Make a list of those five people and put it somewhere safe so when you find yourself in a tough position, you can stop, look at your list, and decide who can help you with your problem.

There's nothing wrong with asking for help or feeling like you need some support. Whether you just need someone to talk to or you need some help solving a problem, the grown-ups in your life are there for you. It's only natural for you to get some help from time to time.

So, are you ready to get started and see all the new things you can learn? We're going to talk about lots of major skills to help you be the best person you can be!

Chapter 1: Growing a Champion Mindset

Can you think of one thing that you want to do with your life? Maybe you want to be the best soccer player on your team, or you dream of writing big books when you're a grown-up. Perhaps you want to be a doctor or an astronaut or the next President, or a rockstar.

No matter what you want to do with your life, it takes a lot of perseverance to get there, and that's part of the journey! Think of one person that you look up to. Maybe it's an actor or an author, or a major person in your life. What makes you admire them so much? Do you think it was easy for them to get to where they are?

I'll tell you one thing: Nothing in life worth doing is easy. Every person you look up to who has succeeded has done one thing to help themselves reach their goals: They didn't give up.

In other words, they had a champion mindset.

What is a Growth Mindset?

Building a champion mindset means that you recognize that your brain is always growing, and it means you recognize that you can always improve if you put in the effort. Even the best people had to practice hard to get to where they are. On the one hand, that probably sounds pretty hard, huh? On the other hand, it means that you can do it, too.

Mindsets can be thought of in two ways: fixed and growth. A fixed mindset is the opposite of a growth mindset and means that you believe that you can't get smarter, better, stronger, or faster. It means that you believe you are either born with talent or you're not, and that's that.

A growth mindset, on the other hand, approaches learning as an exercise. Your brain is like a muscle; the more you exercise it with practice and effort, the better it will get. That's why you learn how to do things in school. You probably started with addition and subtraction in math when you were younger, but now you're starting to learn how to multiply and divide. You can learn those new math skills because your brain grows and learns as you practice.

Did you know that your brain is growing constantly? Your brain is full of neurons, which connect to each other and send little bits of information back and forth that help you learn. When you were born, you had 50 trillion connections between your neurons. By the time you're an adult, you'll have *500 trillion*. That's a lot of learning, growing, and developing! And that's why you should choose to believe in a growth mindset. It'll help you learn how to have that champion mindset that will keep you learning, growing, and developing, and it will also keep you practicing even when things are hard.

Rome wasn't built in a day, and neither were you!

Developing a Champion Mindset

If you haven't read *Life Skills for 8 Year Olds*, you missed the first few lessons on how to develop a champion mindset. The skills we talked about in the previous book were:

1. Try new things

2. Be persistent

3. Change how you think about winning and
   learning

Each of these skills will help you start building a foundation for a growth mindset that will keep you learning and developing. Now, let's look at a few more ways that you can grow your mind and your attitude.

Be Curious

Have you ever thought about how people learned everything we needed to know? We weren't born knowing how to build houses, cook, or take care of ourselves. What we were born with, though, is *curiosity*. Have you ever been around a baby before? They're curious about everything around them. They look at you when you talk to them. They grab whatever they can get their hands on, not because they're dumb babies, but because they're *smart* babies. They're learning about the world around them.

Babies learn so much and have an *innate* curiosity. That means that they were born to be curious, and it's that curiosity that helps them to grow as much as they do and learn so much so quickly. From 2 years old to 7 years old, we learn faster than we do at any other age, and those are the ages where we learn the most. We're learning to talk, how to move in the world, and how to interact with other people.

Even though your brain won't grow as fast now as it did when you were younger, it's still learning quicker than a grown-up's brain. Keep that curiosity to help yourself grow. Ask questions when you have them. Seek out answers and experiment with the world around you. Try new things because you want to know what will happen.

Try new things because you just want to learn them.

Try a 30-Day Challenge

A great way to try new things and keep your brain growing and developing is to try a 30-day challenge. It's not long enough for you to try a new sport or an instrument or some other thing just once before you make a decision on if you like it or not because that doesn't give you enough time to really learn it. Can you imagine how silly it would be to try a new video game one time, and the first time you messed up and lost a life, you gave up? It's okay not to be perfect at something. What's important is that you give yourself plenty of time to develop the skills that you'll need to learn.

Choose something you want to learn how to do. Maybe you want to learn how to knit or sew, or maybe you want to try your hand at gardening or cooking or something else. Once you choose something, you have to commit to doing it every day for 30 days.

Each day, record your progress. If you're sewing, maybe ask a grown-up to take a picture of your project each day. If you're learning how to garden, take a picture of your plant each day. If you're trying to learn a new sport, write down how you do each day.

At the end of the 30 days, look at the first day and the last day and see how far you've come, and maybe decide to do another 30 days and see how you do. It's always fun to see how much you grow! And don't forget to share your results with your grown-ups and friends. They'll probably cheer you on, too!

Choose Positive Language

Did you know that how you speak changes how you think? Here's an example for you. Aidan is a boy who has a really hard time with math. He doesn't quite have the hang of multiplication, and he has a test coming up that he has to study for. He complains to his friend that he can't do multiplication because it's too tough, and he's bad at keeping track of all the numbers. He thinks he'll never be good at it because he's too dumb to get it.

Chloe is a girl who's also really struggling with math. Unlike Aidan, she tells herself that all she has to do is keep practicing, and she'll start doing better. She reminds herself that a few years ago, adding numbers together was hard, but she can add *four-digit numbers* now and gets the answer right every time. She tells herself that she might not be good at math *yet*, but she will be soon enough with practice.

Who do you think will do better?

Aidan believes that he can't learn the math, so instead of putting in the effort to really practice, he halfheartedly tries a couple of easy multiplication problems and gets them wrong, so he gives it up. He doesn't do very well on his test, and when his teacher offers to help him at lunch so he can get extra help, he gets angry.

What about Chloe? Well, she keeps practicing, learning her times tables, and uses those plus the strategies her teacher taught her. She asks her mom to help her learn, and after her mom does a few problems with her, she gets one right! Then, she gets another one right and another one until she's almost always getting the right answers.

The difference between the two is that Chloe used positive language. She didn't see getting the wrong answers as her being dumb, she saw it as an opportunity to keep learning from her mistakes, and soon, she did! Aidan isn't dumb like he said he was; he just didn't put in the effort because he told himself that it wasn't worth it.

Whenever you struggle with something, remind yourself that just because you can't do something *now* doesn't mean that you won't be able to do it *later*. What if we never tried to learn because it was hard? Can you imagine? We'd all be giant babies who don't know how to talk, walk, use the bathroom, or do anything but lay in a bed and cry when we want something!

We come into this world as a blank slate without even knowing how to eat. Everything we do now, we learned. Everything you'll be able to do as an adult, you'll learn eventually. You won't just magically know how to do something just because you hit a certain age. That's why we need positive language when talking about things we can't do *yet*. We'll be able to do it if we apply ourselves and keep trying.

Keep a Diary

It might seem kind of silly to write down what you did each day and how you felt, but this is actually a really good way to help get rid of your bad feelings and see lots of progress over time. Your diary doesn't have to be fancy, but writing down how your day went and what you did can help you reflect on it. It can help you to see how your actions affected the day and what you can do differently if you find yourself running into difficult situations. Try to be as detailed as possible and address the who, what, where, when, and how.

Chapter 2: How to Save Money

Money is so important to everyday life as a grown-up, and yet so many kids don't understand how it works, how long it takes to earn, or why they should save it! Saving money is a skill that everyone needs to know, and the more you work on teaching yourself to save, the better you'll do as a grown-up.

Grown-ups save money for all sorts of reasons, like buying a house, going on vacation, or paying for college for their children. Without saving money, it's easy to spend more than you should, and that can get you into all sorts of trouble as an adult. If you spend too much money, you won't be able to pay your bills or for food. Yes, this is boring now, but it's a good habit to get into, and before you know it, you'll be a pro!

Needs Vs. Wants

In school, you've probably talked about wants and needs before. Needs are things that you really do need. They are the basics, like clothes and shoes that fit and are in good condition (but might not be the fancy ones you want), healthy food, and a home.

Wants are things that are extra. They're nice to have, and you might *really want* them, but you won't get sick or hurt if you don't have them. These are things like that fancy shirt you really want or the new bicycle you've been wishing for, or the newest video game that came out.

When you are a grown-up and responsible for your expenses, you'll have to pay for all your needs. You'll have to pay for your home, a car, food, and all the bills like water (yes, water costs money to use!) and electricity. Your parents probably have a budget somewhere that keeps track of all the needs they have to spend money on each month so they know how much money they have to spend and how much money they can use for fun things they want. It's always important to pay for the needs first and then decide how much money is left for wants after.

Set Financial Goals

Is there something that you've really wanted and been asking for, but your parents have told you no when you've tried to get them to buy it? Maybe it's that new video game system or a tablet, or a LEGO set that you really want.

Everything in this world costs money, and sometimes, that means we have to save for the things we really want.

Talk to your parents about setting a financial goal to save for an item that you want. You might have to do chores, sell things, or do jobs for your neighbors to start making money, but as you do, you'll be able to start saving up for it. Let's say you want the newest video game that came out. Most video games run around $60 these days, plus tax. If you get $9 per week, $1 for every year old you are, how long would you have to save to buy it?

If you did the math, you'd know you need to save for seven weeks to have $63. But, when you buy things from stores, you also have to pay tax. That could be another $5 or $6, depending on where you live, so even after 7 weeks, you'd be a little short. If you saved every penny you got, you'd have to save up for 8 weeks if you get $9 per week. Think you could do it? Perhaps you can find a way to make more than $9 per week so you can reach your goal even faster?

Before we move on, write down one thing that you want to buy and find out how much it costs. Then, talk to your parents about saving up for that one item to see how long it will take you based on how much money you get. If you don't get an allowance, talk to your parents about setting one up for chores. Otherwise, there's always the old-fashioned way by running a lemonade stand or any other hustle you want to do!

Write Down How Much You Spend

If you already get an allowance or you get money on holidays or your birthday, do you track how much money you spend when you do? It's easy to spend, spend, spend without actually thinking about how much something costs until suddenly, you don't have any money left. Writing down how much you spend when you do helps you keep track of how much money you have and helps you to spend wisely.

Imagine you got $100 on your birthday from everyone who came to your party. What would you do? Before you run off to the store to buy the latest toys and games, you should think about how much money you already have and think about how much each item you buy costs.

Let's say you buy ice cream, a candy bar, a cool new action figure, some trading cards, and a video game at the store and use up most of your money, but you don't really pay attention to how much it costs. The next time you go to the store, you won't know how much you have, so when you start reaching for things, you find out that you can't pay for it all and have to put it back.

Writing down how much you spend and then how much money you still have left will help you keep track of your shopping. It can also show you if you're spending money on things that aren't worth it to you, like if you decide that getting a big scoop of ice cream at the ice cream shop isn't worth it when you could buy a big tub of it at the store instead and have it longer.

Saving Money

An important need that should be on any budget is a savings line. You never know when a big expense will pop up when you're a grown-up, and it's good to have money set aside to cover those emergency situations. For example, if you throw a baseball that breaks your neighbor's car's window, your parents will probably have to pay for that, even if they didn't expect it to happen.

As a kid, you probably aren't responsible for paying for sudden expenses like a broken window or a shoe that got eaten by your dog that needs to be replaced. Even so, it's important to get used to saving money now so that when you're older and working, you do it out of habit.

Grown-ups are told that they should save 20% of their money before they start paying for wants and needs. When you get money, your parents might have other rules for you about how much you need to save. Put it away in a piggy bank or save it in a bank or somewhere safe. When you're older, you'll learn about investing so your money can grow on its own, even when you're asleep!

Chapter 3: How to Speak Up for Yourself

Have you ever found yourself in a situation where you feel like you can't speak up? Maybe you're afraid to answer a question in class because you don't know it. Sometimes, you can feel afraid of speaking up for yourself if someone bullies you or if you feel like something is unfair because you think it's easier to stay quiet. If you're quiet when someone does something you don't like, you can get it over with quicker.

The problem is, you shouldn't be in positions where you think you have to ignore how you really feel about something to make other people feel better or to make other people like you more. Speaking up for yourself is all about setting boundaries and enforcing them.

If you've never heard of enforcing boundaries, here's an example. If you don't want your little brother or sister touching your head or playing with your hair, and you say, "No, don't touch me!" then you're enforcing a boundary. Your boundary is that you don't want to be touched.

Your parents probably have boundaries for you, too. There are things that you aren't allowed to do in your family rules, like maybe talking back or not cleaning up your messes when you make them. Your family has boundaries that are enforced if you don't follow them.

Even though you're still a kid, you're allowed to have boundaries. They're healthy to have, even with friends and family members, and if someone tells you that you aren't allowed to have boundaries, you should speak to your trusted grown-ups about it.

What Are Good Boundaries?

Good boundaries are rules that you set for yourself, your body, and your belongings. One of the earliest boundaries you were probably taught was that it's unacceptable to hit other people. Your body is your own, just like other children's bodies belong to them. If you hit someone else, you are pushing yourself onto them, and that can often hurt more than just the impact of hitting.

Empathy is a big part of respecting other people's boundaries. When you have empathy for other people, you understand things from someone else's perspective. We'll talk about this more later, but for now, what you need to know is that the Golden Rule from kindergarten applies here. Treat others the way you want to be treated. That means respecting other people's boundaries just like you want your boundaries to be respected, too.

Some good boundaries that you can set are things like:

- When you can and cannot be touched by others

- Who you spend time with

- What you choose to do

- Who can touch or use your belongings

- Whether you change your mind about something

- How people talk to you

Make a list of some of the boundaries that you have so we can start planning strategies to enforce them. By practicing enforcing your boundaries on your own, it'll be easier when you do have to speak up for yourself.

How to Speak Up to Enforce a Boundary

When someone does something that bothers you and crosses one of your boundaries, being able to speak up for yourself helps you to stand up for yourself and teaches people around you that they can't ignore your boundaries.

Let's talk about Josh and Mia for a minute. Josh and Mia are brother and sister. Josh likes to try to prank his little sister with tricks like putting a toad in her bed or making fun of her when she plays with her dolls. One day, Josh comes into her room to try to give her a big wedgie, and Mia turns around and tells him, "No! I don't like that, don't touch me right now."

Mia enforced a boundary. She told her brother that she did not want to be touched and wanted her personal space. It wouldn't matter if Josh wanted to give her a hug or do something nice to her. If she says no, she is enforcing a boundary.

Speaking up is your first line of defense for your boundaries, and you do it by clearly stating what is and is not okay with you. Protecting your boundaries is something that might take a lot of practice, especially if you're shy, but learning to tell other people when you are uncomfortable is important. Just because you are a kid still doesn't mean that anyone bigger or older than you can tell you what to do, put you down, pick on you, or even touch you.

By clearly saying that you don't like something, you give the person crossing your boundary the chance to empathize with you. You let them know what you are feeling, and then tell them what you do or do not want.

Look at that list of boundaries that you wrote down earlier, and practice what you would say if someone ignored it. Some examples might be:

- "Please don't look at my diary! It's private, and I don't want anyone reading it."

- "Don't take my shirts out of my dresser! They're mine, and I don't want to share right now."

- "I don't want to talk right now. I want to be alone. Please leave me alone right now."

What to Do if Your Boundary Is Crossed and Ignored

Sometimes, even if you enforce a boundary, someone will ignore it. When this happens, it's time to get a grown-up involved. Let's go back to Josh and Mia for a minute. Josh laughs at his sister and says, "Don't be so sensitive! It's just a joke. It's funny. You're being a baby about it." Then, he gives her the biggest wedgie of her life while laughing at her when she runs away.

In this case, Mia goes to get her mother and tells her what happened. She explains that Josh had been teasing her, calling her names, and then he gave her a wedgie when she said she wanted to be left alone. Because using her words didn't work, it's time to get someone else involved. Josh gets in trouble for his behavior and doesn't try to give her a wedgie again.

When you're young, it's hard to get people older than you to listen to boundaries, but that doesn't mean that you shouldn't have them. Your trusted grown-ups are there to help you whenever you need them to keep you safe. Sometimes when it's time to get a grown-up involved are:

- When someone's being too rough even when you asked them to be gentler

- When someone doesn't care what you say and wants to cross your boundary anyway when you say no
- When you feel like the situation is unsafe or you feel uncomfortable with something

- When you're afraid to try to enforce a boundary

Even if the people crossing your boundaries tell you not to get an adult involved, it's important to do it anyway. It doesn't make you a tattletale if you tried to solve the problem yourself first, and it's never okay for someone to push past your healthy boundaries.

Chapter 4: How to Be Safe on the Internet

These days, kids your age are on the internet far more than they were back when I was a kid. You need the internet to do practically anything these days, and because of that, it's important to know how to be safe online. Not everyone on the internet is safe to talk to, and not everything you read is true. That's why it's important to follow your grown-up's rules for using the internet. It keeps you safe because grown-ups will spot the danger sooner than a kid would.

On the internet, it's also possible to be cyberbullied, especially as you get older and start venturing into the world of social media. There are also things on the internet that are inappropriate for kids your age.

Look for the S for Safety

Have you noticed that on websites, the URLs have http:// at the beginning? Well, safe websites have an extra letter there that tells you the website is safe. The letter "s" at the end tells you that the website is secure and protects the information on the website. When playing on the internet, if you don't see "https://" at the beginning of the URL, stay away from it. It could be dangerous.

Never Share Personal Information on the Internet

While you might have to share some personal information on your school websites or while doing schoolwork, the general rule on the internet is not to share anything that identifies you as you. It's too easy for people to find you if you give out more information.

Some information should never be given out over the internet without first asking your parents if it's okay to share. This includes:

- Your full name

- Your birthday and age

- Where you live

- Information about your parents, like their names, jobs, or contact information

- Your phone number, email address, or any other contact information

- Pictures of you

Protect this information and don't share it freely to keep yourself and your family safe. Lots of people on the internet will lie to try to get this information, and that's not okay.

Don't Talk to Strangers on the Internet

When you're talking to people on the internet, remember, you never know who they actually are. It's easy for grown-ups to pretend to be kids on the internet while talking to you, and usually, grown-ups trying to talk to children are up to no good. Whether you're playing games online or just browsing the internet, it's never okay to talk to people that your grown-ups haven't approved.

If you want to be able to talk to your friends or family members, talk to your grown-ups first to find out a way to do it safely. They can help set you up on chats that they have approved so you know that you are safe.

Once It's on the Internet, It's There Forever

An important thing to remember when you're on the internet is that once it's online, you can't really make it disappear again. On the internet, things can be downloaded and saved. Even after you delete pictures and messages, it is still possible to dig them up again, especially for grown-ups who are really familiar with computers. This means that you'll want to be careful not to put anything on the internet that you wouldn't be okay with being there forever.

Don't Do Anything You Feel Like You'd Have to Hide From Your Grown-Ups

Another good rule to remember is that if you ever feel like something you're doing needs to be hidden from your grown-ups, or if you're talking to someone who tells you not to tell a grown-up about something you did or talked about, you probably *should* go get a grown-up. You might be afraid to tell them the truth or what's going on, but they are there to protect you. Their rules are there to keep you safe, and if you're breaking those rules, it's possible that you're doing things that could be dangerous.

Trust that your grown-ups want what's best for you, and that's why they have the rules they do. You probably wouldn't go wandering off in a crowded place without them. Being on the internet is the same thing. It's too easy to get lost, stumble upon things you shouldn't, or meet people who you shouldn't be talking to when you're on the internet and ignoring the rules about it.

Chapter 5: How to Treat a Wound

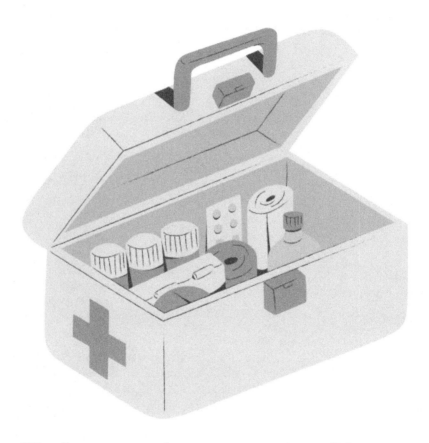

We all get cuts and scrapes sometimes. It's a part of life when our skin can be so delicate. As a young kid, your grown-ups probably took care of your wounds for you to make sure they didn't get infected and healed correctly. As you get older, it's okay for you to take on more of those jobs to take care of them yourself. It can seem pretty scary to take care of a cut that's bleeding, but if it's not very bad, then you should be able to clean it up, bandage it, and care for it until it's healed up.

Caring for a Bleeding Wound

Your skin is your body's first defense against the germs in the world around you. Everything has germs, and when your skin is damaged, those germs can get inside the cut and can cause an infection. Lots of infections won't go away unless they are treated with medicine to fight them off, and they can get worse before they get better, so it's always better to prevent the infection if you can.

The best way to prevent an infection is by keeping your wound clean. Before you touch your wound, make sure your hands are clean and gather up your supplies. You'll want a clean cloth (a clean paper towel or toilet paper will usually work here, too), access to a sink, antibiotic cream or ointment, and a bandage.

1. Put pressure on the wound to stop the bleeding. Don't press hard enough that it will hurt, and make sure whatever you're using to press onto the cut is clean. For most small injuries, this shouldn't take long before your blood clots and stops the bleeding.

2. Wash the wound in the sink with cool water to clean out anything that might have gotten into it, like dirt if you tripped and skinned your knee. If you can't get the body part into a sink to rinse it, you can use a clean cloth with water to do this too.

3. Clean around the wound with mild soap and a clean cloth. Be careful not to get the soap into your actual wound, as it can sting.

4. Spread an antibiotic ointment or cream over the wound, and then put a bandage over it. The bandage will help to keep

germs from getting into your wound to stop infections from forming.

5. Take care of your wound while it heals. Change your bandage whenever it gets wet or dirty, and always change it at least once per day, even if it's kept clean.

Caring for a Burn

Burns are treated a little differently than open, bleeding wounds, but as long as it's just a minor one, you should be able to take care of it just fine. One thing to remember is that with burns, lots of grown-ups (myself included!) were taught that the injury should go under cold water to sort of counterbalance the heat that caused the burn in the first place, but we know better now. Burns should be cooled off with lukewarm water instead of cold water. The cold might feel soothing at first, but it can actually make the injury worse, so it's better to stick to room temperature whenever possible.

If you burn yourself on something hot and it's not that bad of a burn, then treating it is usually pretty simple. Make sure you have a burn cream and a bandage big enough for the injury, and always make sure you wash your hands before handling it at all. If a blister pops up, *do not pop it.*

1. Make sure that your hands are thoroughly washed before starting.

2. Cool your wound in lukewarm water for at least 10 minutes to help the tissue that was burned return back to its normal temperature. This will help with the pain too.

3. Place a burn cream or aloe vera lotion onto the burn, then bandage it up to keep the skin safe.

4. Take care of the burn while it heals by reapplying lotion and putting a bandage over the wound again every day until it goes away. Don't forget to not pop the blister!

When to Ask for Help

Signs a Grown-up Needs to Help With the Wound

Sometimes, the wound is too big for you to treat by yourself, and it might need care from a doctor to heal all the way. These are some times when you should ask your grown-up for help:

- When the wound bleeds when you apply pressure for longer than five minutes

- When the cut is longer than half an inch long or seems deep

- If the wound is on your face or neck
- If the wound was caused by a bite or a puncture wounds (meaning you got poked and stabbed, like if you fell on a stick or a pencil and it poked into you)

- If the burn is worse than a blister or bigger than your pinky

Signs You Might Have an Infection

Other times, your wound can get infected, and you'll need help from a doctor or a grown-up to help clear it up so it can heal. If you notice these signs, it's time to ask for help:

- The area around the wound is getting redder, warmer, and bigger

- The wound is swelling

- You see pus or something cloudy coming out of the wound

- The wound hurts more after two days than it did when it happened

- You feel sick a few days after the wound

- You start getting a fever

Chapter 6: How to See Something From Someone Else's Perspective

We've already talked a little bit about empathy earlier in the book. It's the idea that you understand someone else's *perspective*, meaning that you put yourself in someone else's shoes to imagine what they would think or feel about a situation. This skill helps you to think about other people and how what you do impacts them, too.

Everyone sees the world from different perspectives. We all experience events differently, and we also can't read each other's minds. You might mean well when you do something, but if it bothers the other person, it's important to understand why it bothers them and how you can fix the situation in the future so you can respect them and their boundaries.

Let's go back to Josh and Mia for a second. When Josh gave Mia a wedgie, he did it without thinking about her feelings. When Josh pranks Mia, he ignores her feelings. He thought it was funny to pull those pranks, even though to Mia, they felt mean. Josh didn't look at his actions with empathy and didn't consider how she would react.

Why We Need Empathy

Just like a rock that you throw into a puddle, everything you do has ripple effects on the people around you. Whether you eat the last banana or choose to go to bed instead of spending family movie night together, your actions will touch everyone else. That's why we need empathy. It helps us connect to other people and build good relationships. It also helps us to learn how to act in ways that benefit more than just ourselves.

Josh acted in a way that only benefited himself. He got a laugh out of picking on his sister, but she was the one left feeling upset when he did things that bothered her. Talking about our feelings and how our actions affect those around us helps us to recognize empathy and that everyone and their boundaries around us are important.

Can you think of a time that you empathized with someone? Maybe you did something, and after, realized it upset the other person, and you felt bad. For example, maybe you were playing catch with your best friend, and when you threw the ball a different way, trying to be silly, it hit them in the head, and they got angry about it. If you felt bad for your actions because they hurt someone else, even accidentally, you are empathizing. Or, if your pet whines for food and you feel bad for them because you know how you feel when you're hungry, you're empathizing.

Empathy will help us to work together in ways that benefit everyone, not just ourselves. When we all work together as a team, trying to make sure that everyone benefits and is happy through compromises and cooperation, we make better friends and have better relationships.

How to Develop Empathy and Perspective-Taking

If you feel like empathy is something difficult for you, don't worry! It is a skill that takes a lot of time to build. In fact, boys and girls continue to learn empathy well into their teen years! If you still have room to grow to be more empathetic with people around you, it's important to see that everyone your age does. Girls tend to learn and develop empathy quicker than boys do. They learn to understand perspective-taking more completely around age 13, while boys often take until 15 or 16 to get better at empathizing.

That doesn't mean that you should forget about understanding other people's perspectives. It's something that you should continue to practice as much as possible to make the last part of empathy development easier as you grow up. Practicing helps to make you a better person, friend, and teammate.

Empathizing With Characters

Do you like to read, watch movies, or play games? Characters are often very important parts of all of these. We watch the characters work through challenges and learn how to overcome them. Do you understand how the characters feel when you're watching a movie or reading a book? If you do, that's a type of empathy.

The next time you're interacting with a story, whether it's a game, a book, or a movie, think about what the main character is doing and how they feel. You'll get lots of insight that can help you to identify the feelings that character has, like the way they talk, what they say, and how they act. If you read a book and the character has their arms crossed and a big scowl, you can probably say they're feeling annoyed or angry. Or, if someone is grinning widely, bouncing on the balls of their feet, you'll probably pick up on them being excited.

After you've practiced empathizing with the main characters, it can be fun to do this with a twist by thinking about empathizing with the villain, too. Even though villains are the bad guys in the story, they usually have reasons for doing what they do, and understanding their perspective is a great exercise in practice. After all, if you can empathize with a villain in a story, it should be easier to empathize and take the perspective of someone you are arguing with.

Thinking About Other People's Reactions

Another good activity to help you learn how to look at things from other perspectives is to stop and think about how other people react. The next time you do something for someone else, think about how they responded to you and what you did. Does it make sense that they'd respond the way they did?

For example, if you decide to clean up a room to help your grown-up out, what do you think their reaction will be? Does their reaction align with how they responded? A lot of grown-ups would really appreciate getting some help without asking for it.

On the other hand, if you've done something recently that upset someone else, can you see why they felt the way they did? Maybe you ate an extra bowl of cereal for breakfast, and because you did, there was no milk left when your grown-up went to make some coffee. Can you understand why they'd be upset if you get extra when you normally only get one bowl?

Thinking about how other people respond to you helps you to recognize their perspective. You can walk through *why* they felt the way that they did by imagining how you'd feel in their situation. Would you be disappointed if your sibling took the last of the milk to have extra when you got none? Would you be happy if someone helped you with your chores, so you didn't have to do them? Start practicing predicting how people will react to what you do before you act and see how much easier it gets to connect and interact with people.

Chapter 7: How to Apologize

We all do things that upset or bother people sometimes, even if we don't mean to. If you say something that makes someone unhappy or something that impacts other people, stopping to apologize helps you to reconnect with the other person and fix the problem.

Apologizing is more than just telling someone you're sorry if you upset them. Yes, that's technically saying sorry, but it doesn't acknowledge your responsibility for the situation. It doesn't acknowledge how you'll fix the problem, and it doesn't acknowledge what you'll do so it's not a problem again some other time.

When you apologize to someone in a genuine way, it helps to repair the damage caused by an action. That damage isn't always a big deal. For example, if you break a rule, your grown-ups will probably be upset. That's normal and to be expected. But that doesn't mean that you should be breaking rules or refusing to change your behavior.

A good apology goes a long way in helping mend things and showing the other person that you understand their perspective and that you acknowledge that you did something that upset them.

Why Apologies Are Important

Apologies show that you take responsibility for your actions and also that you empathize with other people. By expressing this, you become more self-aware, a skill that you'll need as you grow. Being self-aware means that you can reflect on your actions and see where they are right or wrong. It means being able to understand what to do differently and how to improve and grow as a person. It's part of having a champion mindset.

With that said, it's also something that can take a lot of practice. If you've never learned how to make a good apology to the people around you, now's as good a time as any to start learning.

Bad Apologies

When you do something wrong, it can be easy to slip into trying to justify what happened. This means that you blame something else for the reason that someone is upset, and you push the responsibility away. If you've ever used the word "but" in an apology, you really just made an excuse and blamed other things for your actions.

Let's go back to Josh and Mia again. After Mia told her mom what happened, Josh had to apologize. He said, "I'm sorry, but it really was just a funny joke! She's too sensitive. My friends wouldn't have gotten mad like that." Do you think that was a good apology?

No!

There are lots of reasons that wasn't a very good apology, starting with the fact that Josh used the word "but" in it. Anything that came after meant he didn't take responsibility. He doesn't recognize that his actions are what upset her in the first place. He thinks it was Mia's fault she got upset and that he got in trouble.

Let's look at another apology. Josh could have said, "I'm sorry you felt that way, Mia. It was just a joke."

Is that a good apology?

No!

The problem this time is that Josh didn't apologize for his actions. He apologized for Mia's feelings. Again, that's not taking personal responsibility and isn't making it clear that he feels bad about how his actions made her feel.

Bad apologies always shift the blame and responsibility away from the action and might even try to make the action or consequence of that action seem smaller than it really was. This is called minimizing.

With that in mind, let's look at what makes a good apology and how to use them.

How to Apologize the Right Way

Good apologies have four steps: They acknowledge or recognize what you did wrong. They express why it was wrong. They express how you will do something different, and they ask for forgiveness and offer to help fix the problem. The next time that you have to apologize to someone, remember these steps.

Step 1: Say How You Were Wrong

The best way to apologize is to start by stating what you did wrong. Even if what happened was an accident, express what happened. Maybe you say, "I'm sorry that I spilled water on your book." Even if you accidentally spilled water on the book, it's important to say that you did it and to accept responsibility. If something happens as an accident, it's still okay for you to apologize.

Step 2: Say Why Your Action Hurt

The next step is to acknowledge why or how what you did could be seen as hurtful. If you spill water on someone's book, you want to show an understanding of why they're upset. "I didn't mean to spill the water, but I know you really like your books, and I should have kept my water at the kitchen table instead of bringing it into the living room to drink on the couch."

By phrasing it like this, you show that you accept responsibility for your actions and that you aren't blaming anyone else for what happened.

Step 3: Say How You'll Do Something Different

The third step is expressing what you'll do differently next time to prevent it from being a problem. This helps you to take personal responsibility because it shows that you understand how your actions caused the problem in the first place. Be specific when you say what you'll do next time. It's not enough to say, "I won't spill water on your book again," because you didn't mean to spill the water this time, either. You're not changing your actions by saying you won't accidentally spill water because accidents can happen at any time.

Instead, you should say something like, "Next time, I'll keep a bottle of water if I'm in the living room, and I'll leave my cups in the kitchen, so I don't spill again." This gives you a plan that you can use to make sure that the problem doesn't come up again.

Step 4: Ask for Forgiveness

Finally, end your apology by asking for forgiveness and asking how you can help fix the problem now. When you make a mistake, it's important to ask for forgiveness. Grown-ups should do this too. And if you did something on purpose that hurt someone else, it's also important to ask for forgiveness and to express that you won't do something similar in the future.

Say something like, "Can you forgive me? And how can I help fix the problem?" By offering to help in the moment, you show that you care about the other person's feelings and that you want to make things right for them.

It might take you a while to get used to apologizing in the right way, but with practice, you'll have it down in no time.

Chapter 8: How to Show Gratitude

Just like how apologies are important to keeping good relationships, showing gratitude also helps you to be a good friend. Having gratitude is being thankful for something. It's that feeling you get when someone does a nice thing for you or helps you out, like a stranger holding a door open at the store or someone offering to help you carry something heavy.

When you have gratitude, you appreciate the effort that someone put into making you happy. Maybe you're happy about a gift you got or just that someone was there for you. Having gratitude can help you look at things around you in a more positive way that helps you to be happier. When you have gratitude, you can see the silver lining, even in bad situations.

Gratitude also helps with developing empathy. People who are grateful tend to be more positive, and even when they are faced with something unhappy or unkind, they don't try to get even with bullies or people who do things to bother them. Gratitude doesn't make people weak or let them be walked all over when they try to do something. It makes them more empathetic, which keeps them from trying to get back at someone else.

As a result, children who use gratitude tend to be happier and tend to have better relationships. But being grateful is about more than just saying please and thank you. It's about taking time to settle down and truly appreciate what you have and the people around you. Here are some ways you can focus on how to be grateful for what you have all around you.

Making a Gratitude Jar

You've probably heard of piggy banks before, where you put your money in them to save it up. A gratitude jar is pretty similar, but instead of depositing money into it to be used later, you deposit slips of paper where you write something that you are grateful for each day.

Choose a jar or even a plastic zipper baggy if you don't have one handy, and decorate it however you'd like. Then, at the end of each day, before you go to bed, you need to stop and think about whatever happened that day that you appreciated or were thankful for. It could be something like your mom making your favorite dinner, your friend drawing you a picture that you love, or even something as simple as having a roof over your head. It doesn't matter what it is that you're thankful for as long as you acknowledge one thing. Write down what you appreciated, then put it in your jar. Then, when you feel down, like nothing is working out, or you're unhappy, you can go back to your jar and revisit the things that have made you smile.

Make a Thank You Card

Has someone recently done something for you that you really appreciated? It could be a parent or a teacher that helped you with an assignment you were unsure of. Writing a thank you card to give to someone who helped you shows them that you appreciate what they did and makes them feel good, too. Often, putting in the extra effort to create a card feels more special to the person being thanked instead of just telling them how you feel. Even better, they get a little keepsake they can look at whenever they want. The card doesn't have to be anything fancy.

Even a piece of notebook paper with a quick message and a nice doodle can be a great thank you card on the go and help spread your love.

Volunteer and Donate to Help Others

When you're grateful for what you have, you also acknowledge that not everyone is as lucky as you are. If you're grateful for the dinner you ate, for example, you realize there are children your age that live in the same city or town as you who don't have anything to eat. If you're thankful for a new pair of shoes, you know there are children out there who only have old pairs that don't fit their feet anymore.

By volunteering and donating your time, money, or old things to others, you acknowledge that you already have what you need and that other people don't. It's easier to feel grateful for what you already have when you see that there are people dreaming of having the same.

Keep in mind that before you volunteer or donate to help other people, you should always talk to your grown-ups so they can help you to develop a safe plan and so you don't give something away that they don't want you to. Don't forget that you always need that permission from your grown-ups.

Tell People Why You Appreciate Them

While this might not be as long-lasting as giving someone a thank you card, telling someone that you appreciate them and why can really make a difference in someone's day. When someone goes out of their way to help you or make your day easier, you should always tell them that you're thankful for it and let them know why.

Be specific. Tell them exactly how they've helped you and why you're so happy. This helps to acknowledge the person who helped you and makes them feel good, and you feel good, too, when you focus on the good things in life.

Chapter 9: How to Build Trust

Do you know what it means to be trustworthy? If you do, stop and think about the most trustworthy person you know. What do they do that lets them earn and keep that trust? How can you use that information to become a trustworthy person yourself?

Being trustworthy means that people can depend on you. It means you follow through when you say that you'll do something. If you made a list of things that a trustworthy person you know does, you'd probably notice that they have traits like:

- They're honest with you.

- They're respectful of themselves and other people.

- They're consistent.

- They care about you and the people around them.

- They show gratitude when you do something for them.

- They're positive and always try to inspire people to be positive too.

- They do things for people even if it doesn't benefit them.

How can you do those things and be trustworthy, too? It's as easy as starting some new habits, and a lot of those, we've already talked about throughout this book. We've already talked about gratitude, respect, and positivity. The other traits can be kind of hard if you're not used to them, but as you practice, you'll be able to show other people how much they matter to you, too.

Always Do What You Say You'll Do

To start, you want to be consistent and keep your promises to other people. A good way to do this is to not say you'll do something if you don't plan on doing it. If you tell someone that you'll do something just to please them in the moment or to avoid an argument, all that happens is that you end up with that argument later on when you don't follow through.

Have you ever been disappointed by someone not doing what they said they'd do for you?

Maybe your parents promised to do something for you, but then the plans changed. Yes, it's disappointing, and it can make you feel bad. It can also make you not trust someone if it happens all the time. That's because consistency matters. If you say you'll do something, you should always try your best to do it because if you never do it, people won't believe you the next time you mean it. Think about the story of the boy who cried wolf. He didn't promise to do anything, but the more he lied about a wolf, the less people believed him until the wolf actually came. Your actions are the same way. If you say you'll clean your room for a week but never do it, do you really think your grown-ups will trust you the next time you promise to do it? You wouldn't believe them if they didn't do what they promised for a week, so why should they?

If your problem is that you say you'll do things and then find out that you can't, then you should use a strategy that lots of grown-ups use when they work. You under-promise and over-deliver. What this means is that you promise to do less than you plan to do, and then you do it all, so it seems like you went above and beyond. If you say you're going to sweep the floors before you go outside, maybe you do it right away and then have extra time afterward to do what you want. If you have to work on a project at school with classmates, promise to have it done by Monday, but actually finish it on Friday. When you do this and consistently finish something before you say you'll have it done, you show yourself as trustworthy because then you're always following through with your promises.

Choose Kindness

Being kind helps make you trustworthy because people can trust that you'll do things to make it easier for everyone, not just yourself. If you have two cookies and your friend has none, sharing one with them shows them that you have their best interests in mind and that you care about how they feel. No, you don't have to share, but choosing to help makes other people think that they can rely on you when they need you because you help them or choose to make them happy even when you don't have to.

By choosing kindness, you also make yourself a more likable person. Part of this goes back to gratitude and positive thinking. Kindness, like gratitude and positivity, is contagious. When you're kind to other people, they want to be kind to you, too. This helps you make friends who trust and care about you.

Listen Well

Have your parents ever sat on their computer or phone while you tried to talk to them? They might be nodding or saying, "That's cool!" while you try to talk, but you know they're not listening, right? How do you feel when that happens? If you're like me, that makes you feel bad and like the things that you have to say don't matter at all.

Choose to listen well and pay attention to what people say to you when they come to talk. Stop what you're doing and talk to them. Ask them questions about what they're talking about and engage in the conversation. Doing this also shows them that they matter to you, which makes you seem more trustworthy since they know they can come to you to talk if they need to.

Good listening means that your whole attention is on the person talking. It means that you're hearing what they're saying instead of trying to come up with responses to them. When you listen well, you connect more with the other person and if you listen during a conflict, you can both work together to solve it on your own.

Be Honest

Finally, to help yourself become trustworthy, you should always choose honesty. Now, this doesn't mean you can be mean if you don't like someone or something, but you should be truthful when you're asked about something.

The trick here is finding a kind way to say your truth. If your friend asks you if you like their shirt and you really, really don't, there are kind ways that you can say this. For example, you could say, "I know you really like that shirt, and I can see how happy it makes you!" There's no reason for you to say, "No way, that shirt makes you look ugly!" when that's a hurtful way to share your opinion.

Honesty is also important if you do something wrong. It's part of taking responsibility, as we talked about earlier when discussing apologies. Be honest on your part if you do something wrong and take responsibility for it. People may be upset that you did something they didn't like, but showing them that you can take responsibility makes you reliable, and that's something people care about.

Chapter 10: How to Be Safe When You're Alone

When you go out with your grown-ups, do you pay much attention to the world around you? You probably look at what's going on, or if you're at a store, you might have fun looking at all the items, but are you paying attention to the people around you? A lot of children don't. They trust that their parents do that for them, even if it's not something that they really think about.

As you are getting older, you may start asking about staying home alone, or you might go to play outside by yourself with your friends in the neighborhood. You might even be getting close to the age where your parents will let you start walking to and from school or the bus stop by yourself.

But, as you start going out by yourself, you don't have your grown-ups' watchful eyes on you anymore, and you have to take the responsibility to watch out for yourself instead. That's why you have to learn how to be safe when you're alone.

Learning About Situational Awareness

Situational awareness is a fancy way of saying you're aware of what's going on around you. It means paying attention to the people nearby, the cars passing, and what other people are doing. If you're going to be outside by yourself, or if you're staying home alone when your grown-ups go somewhere, it's important to be aware of these things because you don't have anyone else to do it for you. If you want to cross the street, you have to know it's safe before you do. If you want to play with your friends, you need to be aware of strangers.

A way that you can learn situational awareness is to practice playing spy games with your friends or by yourself. The next time you're outside, look at every person that passes and try to remember the colors of their shirts. If you notice someone standing nearby and watching you or your friends, pay attention to who they are.

Another part of situational awareness is having a plan for if something goes wrong or something doesn't feel right. If you feel like a situation is uncomfortable, it's important for you to trust yourself and that feeling. You have that instinct to be afraid in dangerous situations to keep yourself safe. If you get that feeling, the best thing you can do is get to a trusted grown-up as quickly as you can and tell them about it.

Stranger Danger

You've probably heard the phrase "Stranger danger" a lot growing up, and even though you're older now, it's still important. Some grown-ups are unsafe, and they count on kids not knowing better when they try to take them. Any stranger that you don't know should be avoided. Pay attention to strangers that follow you or try to get you to go over to their cars because this is unsafe.

If you have a cell phone or a smartwatch that you can use to contact your grown-ups when you're away from them, you should always do so when you notice that someone seems to be following you around or if they try to talk to you and get your attention or try to get you to follow them.

If a stranger insists on you going with them, it's okay to make a scene. It's okay to yell, "I don't know you, go away and leave me alone!" Other adults who are minding their own business will probably look and try to see what's going on if the stranger insists on talking to you.

If you have to get help and your grown-up isn't around, looking for someone in a uniform, like a police officer or firefighter, can help you. If you can't find someone in a uniform, try to find someone else with kids with them and ask for help. Most people in this world are good, and if someone is leaving you alone and doing their own thing, they may be able to help you out of a messy situation. It's the strangers that try to force you to listen or talk to them or go with you that you should avoid as much as possible.

What to Do if Someone Tells You They Know Your Grown-Ups

Sometimes, strangers with bad ideas will try to tell you that they know your parents or grandparents and give you a story about how they were told to go get you and bring you back to them. Before you think it's a good idea to go with them, you should stop and think about if your parents would really send a stranger to go get you without telling you first. They probably wouldn't.

A good way to avoid this is to come up with a password that you use with your parents when you need help or when they need you to know that someone is safe to go with. Choose something that no one would ever guess, like "Peanut butter waffles with chocolate chips" or a silly phrase, and let that be your password with your parents. If your parents really sent someone to go get you, they'd give that person your password, and you'd know they were telling the truth.

If you can call your parents to ask them if it's safe, that's always a good idea, too. The point is to make sure that you aren't going with a stranger who doesn't have a reason to be talking to you.

Chapter 11: How to Talk to a Grown-Up When Someone Tells You to Keep a Secret

Secrets might seem harmless, but they can be really dangerous. If someone asks you to keep a secret, you should immediately stop and think about why they'd want to do or say something that they wouldn't want your grown-ups to know, too. You see, there's a difference between secrets, private things, and surprises, even though all three of them involve not telling someone else about them.

Privacy is about respecting what someone tells you in confidence. They tell you something about themselves that they don't want to share with other people. Privacy is different from a secret because it doesn't hurt either person. You might tell your best friend in private that you're really afraid you're going to fail a test, but you don't want other people to know about it. Keeping that private isn't going to hurt anyone, and it's about trust.

Surprises are kind of like secrets because it means that you're going to stay quiet about something. The difference is that surprises are supposed to be positive, and they are temporary. If your mom tells you to be quiet because she bought a present for your dad and wants it to be a surprise, she's not asking you to keep a secret; she's asking you to keep it a surprise. You only have to stay quiet for a period of time before letting the other person in on it. Surprises are safe and positive.

Secrets are different. When someone tells you to keep a secret and not tell your grown-ups about what happened, they are hiding something from the people who are responsible for you. Even if the person telling you to keep a secret is another family member, it's not good to keep them. Usually, secrets are dangerous or harmful. They might even come with threats that the person will try to hurt you or your family if you say something. When someone tells you to keep a secret, and they don't mean that they want to talk to you in private, then you should always go to a grown-up to talk about it. Your parents or other grown-ups are there to help you through situations like these.

Why Secrets Are Bad

Secrets are bad because they try to get you to ignore something that you know is wrong. You have to carry the burden of being told to be quiet or not reach out for help in a situation. It also means that you're being told not to be honest with your family, who you should be able to tell anything to. The grown-ups that take care of you are people you can talk to about anything in this world. They are your safe spot and the people who will be there to help and support you, no matter what.

When someone does something that they don't want your parents to know about, it's because they know that your grownups wouldn't be happy about it. It could be that you went out with a family member and they let you do a whole bunch of things that you're not allowed to do, like ride in the front seat of the car or do something dangerous like playing in a river without a lifejacket.

If the person asking you to keep the secret knows that it's something your grown-ups wouldn't approve of, then it's probably not something that's safe. They might tell you that you'll get in trouble, or that you won't be able to go spend time with them anymore, or put some other consequence on you that makes you feel like you can't tell your grown-ups the truth. This isn't fair for you and if a grown-up is telling you to keep secrets from your parents, then they aren't trustworthy. They're up to something that they know your grown-ups would argue about, and that's not safe or okay.

Telling Your Grown-Ups About Secrets

As soon as someone asks you to keep a secret from your grown-ups, it's important that you tell them as soon as you can. Your grown-ups might be upset, but remember; it's important to be honest if you want to be trustworthy. By telling your grown-ups about what happened, you help yourself to stay safe.

To start, go up to your trusted adult and tell them that you have to talk to them. Then, it's time to be completely honest. Depending on the secret, your grown-ups may be angry, upset, frustrated, or have some other negative emotion, and that's okay.

If your parents ask questions after you tell them the secret, it's important to answer them honestly, so they understand who told you to keep a secret and why. This information helps them to figure out what to do next after you've been told to be quiet.

Chapter 12: How to Talk About Consent

In life, the one thing you always have control over is your own body. As a kid, you probably don't make the rules at home, and you don't get to make decisions about all sorts of things. One thing you always get to make decisions about is your body. Your body is your own, and for the most part, that means that other people cannot touch you if you don't want them to.

Some exceptions to this may be if your parents have to lift you up or move you or if your parents are in the room and say that a doctor can examine you. Otherwise, anyone who wants to so much as give you a hug needs to talk to you beforehand.

When you tell someone that they can give you a hug, you are consenting. Consenting is a fancy word for giving permission, and it often is used to talk about giving permission to other people to be close to you.

Part of giving consent is enforcing your own boundaries. If you don't want to be touched, you are allowed to say no. You're also allowed to say yes, you want a hug. If you want to hug someone else and they tell you no, then you have to respect that, too.

Personal Space and Bodily Autonomy

Everyone has their own bodily autonomy; this means that we all have a say over our own bodies. You can't decide to touch someone else, and someone else can't choose to touch you, either. Just as you want your boundaries to be respected, it's important that you give that same respect to those around you as well. When you respect other people's bodily autonomy, you respect their boundaries and show that you are trustworthy.

Personal space and bodily autonomy are two lessons that should always be respected. The more that you respect other people's boundaries and enforce your own, the more that you and other people come to trust each other.

One way to enforce your physical boundaries is to tell people what you want. If grandma comes over and tells you to give her a hug, but you really don't want a hug, it's okay to say, "No thanks, I don't want to be touched right now."

Keep any personal contact that you have with other people to things that you are comfortable with. It's okay if you don't always want to be touched.

It can also help if you have a private place you can go to in your home, like your bedroom, if you don't want to be touched and want to be left alone.

Listening to Other People

Of course, you need to respect the boundaries that other people set for you, too. It's okay for other people to choose to enforce a boundary and say they don't want a hug or to be touched or to play a game that would require physical contact, like tag. If your friend, who normally doesn't mind being hugged and touched, says that they want to be left alone and not touched, they do not give you consent to touch them. This means that you have to listen.

You should never try to pressure someone into letting you touch or hug them. They are allowed to have their boundaries, whatever they may be, and you have to respect that. It can be hard to get used to, especially if they've recently changed how much physical touch they are okay with. The most important thing to remember is that if they tell you nicely that they want to be left alone, you really do need to respect it.

No Means No

Whether you or someone else says no, it's time to listen. If you tell someone that you don't want to be touched and they don't listen to you, it's important to go to a grown-up to ask for help. If you told someone no and asked them to stop touching you, whether it was a tickle, a hug, or some other kind of touch, you need to tell a grown-up so they can help you.

Any touches that are unsafe can hurt your feelings or hurt you. These could be touches like someone hitting you, throwing something, or pushing you. Unwanted touches are those that you simply don't want because they make you uncomfortable. Even a hug can be an unwanted touch in a moment if you don't want to be touched at all. If anyone touches you in an unsafe or unwanted way, you need to tell your grown-up. If you touch someone else in an unsafe or unwanted way, the other person needs to tell their grown-up, who will probably talk to you about why it's so important that you listen to consent when other people offer or give it.

Chapter 13: The Importance of Sleep

Sleep is like a magic potion that helps your body and mind recharge, grow, and stay healthy. Just like how showing gratitude and being kind are important, getting enough sleep is essential for you to be your best self. When you sleep, your body is hard at work, repairing itself and preparing you for a new day of adventures, learning, and fun.

Sleep helps you concentrate better, remember things more easily, and even keeps you in a better mood. Have you ever noticed that when you don't get enough sleep, you might have trouble focusing on your schoolwork? That's because sleep is vital for your brain to function optimally.

Sleep helps you think better and be more creative. When you've had a good night's sleep, your brain can come up with new ideas and find solutions to problems more easily. This can help you with schoolwork, making art, writing stories, and even figuring out how to deal with tricky situations like the ones we talked about before. Sleeping well also helps your brain remember and organize everything you've learned during the day, so you can use that knowledge later on.

Getting enough sleep is also important for how you feel. When you're well-rested, it's easier to handle your emotions and stay calm when things get tough. You'll be more patient and understanding with your friends and family, too. Plus, when you've had a good sleep, you can enjoy all the fun and exciting things in life even more.

So, when you make sure you get enough sleep every night, you're helping your body, mind, and feelings stay healthy and strong. You're also giving yourself the chance to be more creative, solve problems, and feel good about the world around you. Sleep is really important for living a happy, balanced, and exciting life.

Now, let's take a look at how much sleep you need, how to make sure you're getting enough of it, and how to fall asleep easily, so you can be at your best every day.

How Much Sleep Do You Need?

As a 9 year old, you need about 8 to 10 hours of sleep each night. You might be thinking, "Wow, that's a lot of time!" But remember, your body is doing important work while you're asleep, so it's important to make sure you give it enough time to get the job done.

Create a Sleep-Friendly Environment

To help you get the best sleep possible, you need to create a cozy and relaxing space for sleeping. Here are a few tips to make your room more sleep-friendly:

1. Keep it cool, dark, and quiet: A cool, dark, and quiet room helps your body relax and makes it easier to fall asleep. Try using blackout curtains or an eye

mask to block out light, and a fan or a white noise machine to reduce noise.

2. Make your bed comfortable: Choose a comfortable mattress, pillows, and blankets to make your bed feel like a soft, cozy nest. You can even have a special stuffed animal or blanket that helps you feel safe and secure.

3. Keep screens out of the bedroom: Watching TV or playing on a tablet or phone before bed can make it much harder for you to fall asleep. So, try to keep screens out of your bedroom and find other relaxing activities to do before bedtime, like reading a book or drawing.

Establish a Bedtime Routine

Having a bedtime routine is a great way to signal to your body that it's time to wind down and get ready for sleep. A routine can also help you relax and make it easier to fall asleep. Here are some ideas for creating your own bedtime routine:

1. Take a warm bath or shower: The warm water can help you feel more relaxed and sleepier.

2. Put on comfy pajamas: Choose soft, comfortable pajamas that make you feel cozy and ready for bed.

3. Read a book or listen to a calming story: Reading or listening to a story can help your mind settle down and prepare for sleep.

4. Practice deep breathing or gentle stretches: Taking slow, deep breaths or doing some gentle stretches can help your body relax and release any tension from the day.

5. Say goodnight to your family: Saying goodnight to your loved ones can help you feel connected and loved, making it easier to drift off to sleep.

By making sleep a priority and creating a sleep-friendly environment, you're setting yourself up for success every day. Remember, getting enough sleep is just as important as showing gratitude, being kind, and taking care of yourself in other ways.

So, sweet dreams, and here's to waking up refreshed and ready for a new day!

Conclusion

Hey, you amazing 9 year old! Congratulations, you made it to the end! If you've been paying attention, you just learned a whole lot of important skills that you'll use for the rest of your life. It might seem silly to think that these things that you learn right now will impact you as a grown-up, but really, growing up is all about learning the things you need to do to take care of yourself. Some of those things aren't very fun, such as learning how to do chores or saving money. Other things might seem like they're for children, like practicing empathizing with characters in stories.

The thing is, these are all things that will affect you, even as a grown-up. Grown-ups have to be able to get along with other people to be good team players at work. They have to be able to learn and grow as people, just like you do. Growing and learning don't stop just because your body stops growing. Your mind will always continue to grow, even as an adult. That's just part of having a champion mindset.

When you have a champion mindset, all of these skills become possible for you to complete because you'll keep trying and working on developing them. You'll recognize that you are capable of growing as a person.

Each day you have is another day that you can start learning something new. Each day is the chance to develop yourself and learn the foundation you need so you will be able to be a good grown-up as you age. Before you know it, you'll be saying goodbye to the childhood years and welcoming the tween and teen ones. Those years bring their own challenges, and these life skills will help you then too.

So, get out there and start putting these skills to good use!

Leave Your Feedback on Amazon

Please think about leaving some feedback via a review on Amazon. It may only take a moment, but it really does mean the world for small authors like myself :)

Even if you did not enjoy this title, please let me know the reason(s) in your review so that I may improve this title and serve you better.

From the Author

As a retired school teacher, my mission with this series is to create premium educational content for children that will help them be strong in the body, mind, and spirit via important life lessons and skills.

Without you, however, this would not be possible, so I sincerely thank you for your purchase and for supporting my life's mission.

118

Don't forget your free gifts!

(My way of saying thank you for your support)

Simply visit **haydenfoxmedia.com** to receive the following:

- 10 Powerful Dinner Conversations To Create Amazing Kids

- 10 Magical Affirmations To Help Kids Become Unstoppable in Life

(you can also scan this QR code)

More titles you're sure to love!

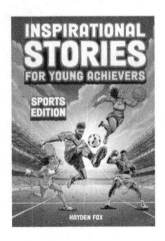

Made in the USA
Las Vegas, NV
03 October 2023

78399561R00069